Cut, Paste, and Create

Cut and Paste

Trucks, Trains, and Big Machines

Rosie Hankin

GARETH**STEVENS**
GS
PUBLISHING
A Member of the WRC Media Family of Companies

Thank you Ottilie, Freddie, Idina, and Sylvia for your help and inspiration.

Please visit our web site at: www.garethstevens.com
For a free color catalog describing Gareth Stevens Publishing's
list of high-quality books and multimedia programs, call
1-800-542-2595 (USA) or 1-800-387-3178 (Canada).
Gareth Stevens Publishing's fax: (414) 332-3567

Library of Congress Cataloging-in-Publication Data available upon
request from publisher. Fax (414) 336-0157 for the attention of
the Publishing Records Department.

ISBN-13: 978-0-8368-7721-2 (lib. bdg.)

This North American edition first published in 2007 by
Gareth Stevens Publishing
A Member of the WRC Media Family of Companies
330 West Olive Street, Suite 100
Milwaukee, Wisconsin 53212 USA

This U.S. edition copyright © 2007 by Gareth Stevens, Inc. Original edition
copyright © 2005 by Haldane Mason Ltd. First published in 2005 by Red Kite Books,
an imprint of Haldane Mason Ltd., P.O. Box 34196, London NW10 3YB, United Kingdom.
(info@haldanemason.com)

All original artwork by Rosie Hankin.

Gareth Stevens editor: Barbara Kiely Miller
Gareth Stevens designer: Kami Strunsee

Printed in Canada

1 2 3 4 5 6 7 8 9 10 10 09 08 07 06

Contents

Craft A-B-Cs

Making things with paper, cardboard, paste or glue, and other craft materials is lots of fun! You will *be* surprised at what *you* can make when *you* start to cut, paste, and create!

Making Cut-and-Paste Crafts!

You can make the fun crafts in this book using simple materials that you cut up and then paste or stick together. To get started, choose a craft, then collect and prepare the materials you need. Next, read through the instructions and look at the picture of the finished project. The picture shows you how to paste all the pieces together to create a work of art. If some steps are too difficult for you, ask a grown-up for help.

You do not need to be an artist to make fun and interesting crafts. You only need to cut and paste different shapes. Each project in this book uses simple shapes such as circles, squares, rectangles, and triangles. The shapes you need for each project are shown in the book. Each shape has a number on it. The number tells you how many pieces of that shape you need to make. The shapes also have names to help you fit them together.

All the shapes are easy to draw or trace. To trace a shape, place a sheet of tracing paper on top of a page in the book. Tracing paper is very thin, white paper you can see through. Use a pencil to draw the outline of a shape on the tracing paper. Cut out the shape you have drawn. Use the shape as a pattern, or template, to draw the shape on colored paper or cardboard. You can make your shape the same size or bigger or smaller than the shape in the book.

4

To make each craft in this book, first draw and cut out all the pieces, then follow the numbered instructions and look at the pictures to learn how to paste or glue them in place. Your finished craft does not have to look exactly like the picture. You can create each craft your own way. Look in the book for **Bright Ideas!** to make your craft even more special.

Shapes such as circles are hard to draw well, but you can find many round objects to draw around: coins, glasses, cups, plates, and bowls. Look around for objects with other shapes, such as ovals, that might be useful in drawing the shapes needed for these projects.

Once you have tried some of the ideas in this book, you will be able to dream up your own works of art.

Look through old magazines and cut out pictures of things to use in your craft projects. A photo of stones was pasted over the back of this truck. You could even put a photo of yourself or a friend in the window of the truck. Never cut up a magazine or a photo, however, without asking a grown-up first!

Craft Materials

For all the crafts in this book, you need a pencil, a ruler, scissors with rounded tips, and white paste, glue, or a glue stick. Each craft has a list of the other materials you will need. Most of the crafts use thick, colored construction paper or thin, colored cardboard. You may also need paper plates and bowls, stickers, and clear tape.

Kinds of Paper

The colored paper and cardboard used for these crafts are the kind you probably have at school or at home. Special kinds of paper are also needed for some of the crafts. Adhesive paper is like a sticker. You peel the adhesive paper away from its paper backing and press it down to make it stick. Tissue paper is thin, soft paper that usually comes in large, folded sheets. Corrugated paper has a lot of ridges and grooves. Crepe paper is stretchy paper that comes in many colors. Aluminum foil is shiny paper that looks like a thin sheet of metal. You probably have aluminum foil in your kitchen.

The instructions for each craft tell you to use certain colors of paper or cardboard, but you can use any colors you like. If the only paper or cardboard you have is white, you can color it yourself with crayons or colored pencils or markers. You can even paint it.

Finding Supplies
. . . .

You do not have to buy all the supplies you need for these projects. You can sometimes find colored paper in old magazines and can use the cardboard from packages such as cereal boxes. Ask your parents if they have scraps of fabric, yarn, and other small items you can use. You can create works of art with things you find lying around your own home, such as cardboard tubes from empty rolls of paper towels or toilet paper. Always ask a grown-up if it is okay to cut up or use any materials before you begin.

Staying Safe
. . . .

To stay safe while you cut and paste, always use scissors with rounded tips when you need to cut things. If you have trouble cutting cardboard with your safe scissors, ask a grown-up to cut it for you with sharper scissors or a knife. Use only paints, felt-tip pens, and glues that are nontoxic, which means they are safe for kids. You may get glue or paint on your fingers, so keep your hands away from your face until after you wash them.

Making a Mess and Cleaning Up
. . . .

Creating crafts almost always means making a mess. Before you begin, cover your work surface with old newspapers or a tablecloth that can be wiped clean. Wear an apron or an old shirt to protect your clothes, and roll up your sleeves. If you are painting, use water bowls with wide bases so they do not tip over. Fill up a sink with warm, soapy water so it is ready for washing your hands, paintbrushes, paint jars, and other tools. When you have finished working, pick up and put away all the materials you were using. Now everything will be ready for the next time you want to cut, paste, and create.

Race Car

You will need:

- red, green, black, and white paper or cardboard
- background cardboard (any color)

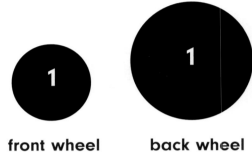

front wheel　　**back wheel**

front hubcap　　**back hubcap**

driver's helmet

1 Draw the shape of the race car body on red paper or cardboard and cut it out.

2 Cut the shape for the driver's helmet out of green paper or cardboard.

3 To make the back and front wheels, draw a large circle and a medium-sized circle on black paper or cardboard. Use coins or other small, round objects to help you draw the circles. Cut out the circles.

race car body

8

This picture of the race car shows how you should paste the pieces together. Are you ready to start your engine? It's time to race!

4 For hubcaps, draw two smaller circles on white paper or cardboard and cut them out.

5 Paste or glue the race car body onto the background cardboard.

6 Paste on the driver's helmet.

7 Paste the black wheels onto the car. Put the bigger wheel at the back.

8 Paste the hubcaps onto the wheels.

Bright Ideas!
• Decorate your car with silver racing stripes.
• Cut a simple flag shape out of white paper. Draw a checkered pattern on the flag, then glue the flag to the background cardboard. Draw in a flag pole. Your car has won!

Tugboat

- blue background cardboard
- turquoise, red, yellow, and black paper or cardboard
- round white stickers

1

upper deck

1

smokestack

1

water

1 Measure the length of the blue background cardboard. Cut a long strip of turquoise paper or cardboard, making it the same length.

2 Cut the shape of the boat base out of red paper or cardboard.

3 Cut a rectangle out of yellow paper or cardboard for the upper deck.

boat base

This picture of the tugboat shows you where to glue all the pieces. Tugboats pull much bigger boats. What will your tugboat pull?

4 Cut out a square piece of black paper or cardboard for a smokestack.

5 Paste the strip of turquoise paper or cardboard along the bottom of the background cardboard. The turquoise strip is the water.

6 Paste the red boat on the water, then paste the yellow rectangle on top of it to make the boat's upper deck. Paste the black smokestack on top of the upper deck.

7 Stick round white stickers on the red boat base the boat to make portholes.

Bright Ideas!
• Cut red stripes to paste on the smokestack and paste windows on the upper deck of the boat.
• Make two sides for your boat. To make the boat stand up, use clear tape or glue to stick one side of the boat onto each end of an empty cardboard box or an empty toilet paper roll.

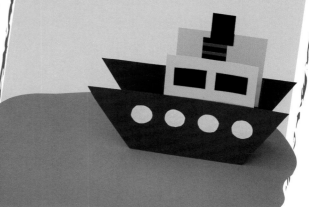

Spaceship

- thick, black felt-tip pen
- blue background cardboard
- aluminum foil
- yellow paper or cardboard
- yellow, orange, and red crepe paper or tissue paper
- star-shaped stickers

1 Use a black felt-tip pen and a ruler to draw a spaceship on the blue background cardboard.

2 Tear aluminum foil into twelve pieces that are each about 4 inches (10 centimeters) square.

3 Cut a triangle out of yellow paper or cardboard.

4 Cut flame shapes out of yellow, orange, and red crepe paper or tissue paper.

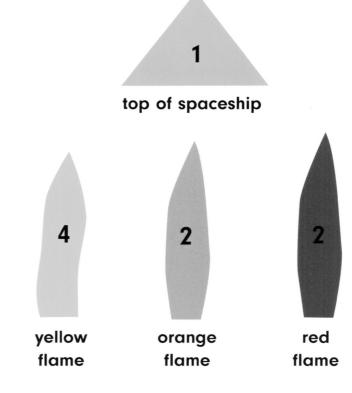

top of spaceship

yellow flame

orange flame

red flame

This picture of the spaceship shows where to glue all the pieces. Your spaceship will soon be ready to blast off to the stars!

Bright Ideas!
- Use black background cardboard and cut the shape of the spaceship out of colored cardboard.
- Cut three exhaust funnels out of a different color of cardboard.

5 Paste the yellow triangle at the top of the spaceship. Paste the flames at the bottom of the spaceship.

6 Loosely scrunch the foil squares into balls and paste them onto the spaceship.

7 Put star-shaped stickers on the background cardboard around the spaceship.

13

Pickup Truck

- red, black, and gray paper or cardboard
- background cardboard (any color)

- round white and yellow stickers
- orange and yellow tissue paper, cut into strips

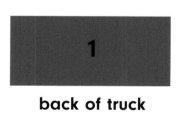
back of truck

1 Cut two rectangles out of red paper or cardboard for the back and front of the truck. Cut one more rectangle for the truck's cab, cutting one end at an angle for the roof.

front of truck

2 Cut circles for wheels out of black paper or cardboard.

wheel

3 Cut a rectangle out of gray paper or cardboard for a window.

cab of truck

window

This picture of the truck shows how you should paste or glue all the pieces together. What will your truck carry? It can be a load of straw — or strawberries!

4 Paste the red shapes for the truck onto the background cardboard.

5 Paste the window on the cab of the truck and paste on the wheels. Stick on round white stickers for hubcaps.

6 Stick a round yellow sticker onto the front of the truck for a headlight.

7 Paste or glue strips of tissue paper over the back of the truck to look like straw.

Bright Ideas!
- Look through magazines for pictures of things to paste over the back of the truck. Your truck could carry stones, logs, candy, or even toys!
- Cut a round black sticker in half to add front and back bumpers.

Shoebox Car

You will need:

- shoebox with a lid
- red paint
- paintbrush
- yellow and black cardboard
- white or silver cardboard or aluminum foil

hubcap

headlight

wheel

1 Ask a grown-up to cut the lid of a shoebox in half.

2 Paste around the inside edges of one half of the lid and glue it over the open side of the shoebox.

3 Paint the box and the half lid with red paint. You can paint the inside of the box, too. Let the paint dry.

4 While the paint is drying, cut two small circles out of yellow cardboard for headlights.

5 Cut four large circles out of black cardboard to make wheels. Cut four small circles out of white or silver cardboard, or out of aluminum foil, for hubcaps.

This picture of the shoebox car shows how to paste all the pieces together. Is your teddy bear ready to go for a ride?

6 Paste a hubcap onto the center of each wheel.

7 Paste the wheels onto the sides of the painted shoebox.

8 Paste the yellow headlights onto the front of the shoebox. The front is the end with the lid on it.

Bright Ideas!
- Cut the front half of the shoebox at an angle to make the front of the car slope downward.
- Cut a circle for a steering wheel out of the unused half of the lid. Paint it the same color as the car. Draw a thick line around the edge of the circle and another thick line across the middle. Put a small, round black sticker in the center, then paste the steering wheel onto the half lid covering the shoebox.
- Cut out a white rectangle for a license plate. Write a license number on the rectangle with a black felt-tip pen.

Airplane

- blue cardboard
- cardboard tube from empty roll of toilet paper
- blue paint

- paintbrush
- 4 large, round red stickers
- 4 small, round black stickers
- 2 adhesive dots

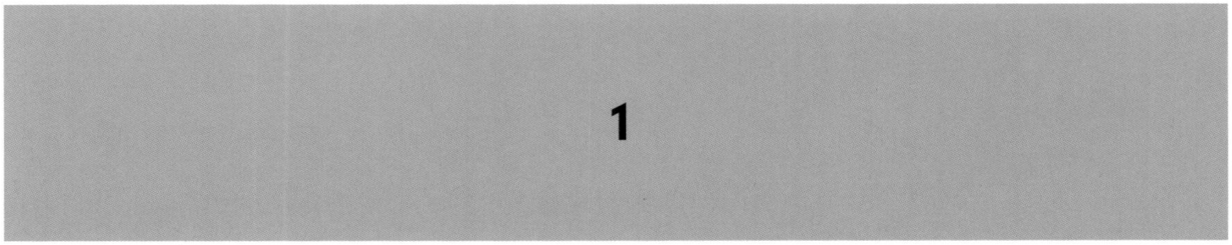

1

front wings

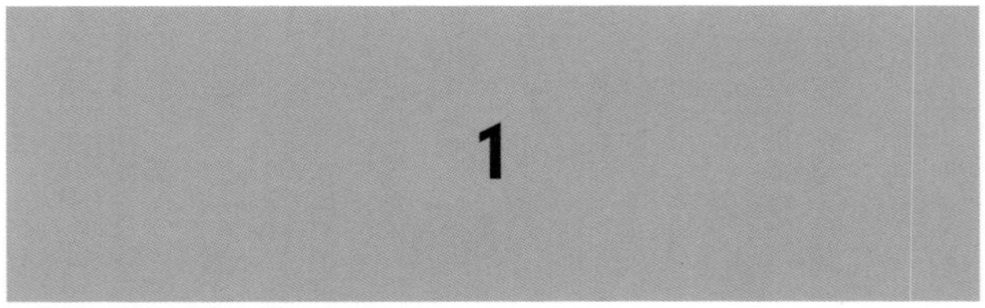

1

tail wings

1 Draw two strips on blue cardboard. Make one strip about 6 inches (15 cm) long and the other strip 3 inches (7.5 cm) long. Cut out both strips.

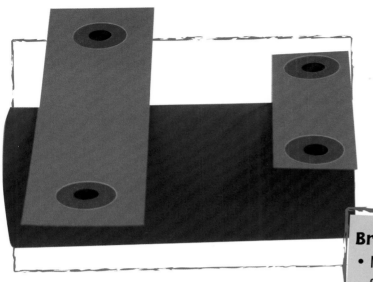

This picture of the airplane shows you how to put all the pieces together. Now your airplane is ready to fly through the sky!

2 Paint the cardboard tube blue. Let the paint dry.

3 While the paint is drying, make the airplane's wings. Stick a red sticker at each end of each strip of blue cardboard. Stick a black sticker in the center of each red sticker.

4 Use paste or adhesive dots to stick the front and tail wings onto the top side of the painted cardboard tube.

Bright Ideas!
- Make a larger plane using the cardboard tube from an empty roll of paper towels. Use thicker cardboard for the wings so they do not bend.
- Add windows cut out of silver paper or foil.
- Make a tail fin by cutting a long, thin strip of cardboard. Fold the strip in half, then fold back two flaps at each end. Paste the sides of the top half of the fin together, then paste the flaps of the fin to the tail wings.

Train

You will need:

- cardboard tube from empty roll of paper towels
- red cardboard
- white paper or cardboard
- cardboard tube from empty roll of toilet paper

- red, yellow, blue, and green paints
- paintbrush
- 1 round black sticker
- black yarn
- clear tape

1 Ask a grown-up to cut the paper towel tube into three equal pieces with a sharp knife.

2 Draw a strip about 9 inches (23 cm) long and 2 inches (5 cm) wide on red cardboard. Cut out the strip.

3 Cut two small squares out of white paper or cardboard. The white squares should be small enough to fit on the red strip.

> **2**
>
> **window**

> **1**
>
> **cab for engine**

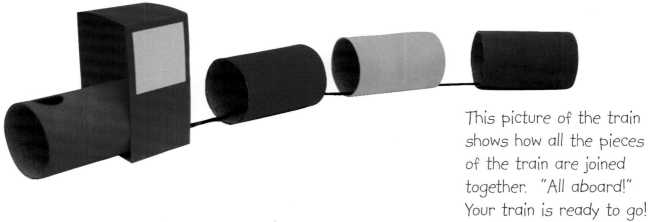

This picture of the train shows how all the pieces of the train are joined together. "All aboard!" Your train is ready to go!

4 Paint a toilet-paper tube red. Paint one piece of paper towel tube yellow. Paint another one blue. Paint the third one green. Let the paint on all four tubes dry completely.

5 Fold the red cardboard strip so it fits around the red tube. This is the cab for the train's engine. Paste one white window onto each side of the cab, near the folds. Paste the cab onto one end of the red tube. Stick a black sticker on the top of the tube, near the front.

6 Thread black yarn through the insides of all the tubes to join the engine and the three train cars. Use clear tape to hold the yarn in place.

Bright Ideas!
- Make straight sides for the train cars using rectangles of colored cardboard.
- Add black stickers to the cars and engine for wheels.
- Cut a circle out of red cardboard for the front of the engine. Use stickers to make lights.
- Use a plastic bottle top for a smokestack.

Monster Truck

- red and black paper or cardboard
- 2 paper bowls
- gray paint
- paintbrush
- background cardboard (any color)
- round yellow sticker, cut in half
- star stickers

1 Draw the shape of the truck body on red paper or cardboard and cut it out.

2 Cut a window shape out of black paper or cardboard.

3 Draw two circles on black cardboard for hubcaps. Make these circles the same size as the flat bottoms on the paper bowls. Cut out the circles.

4 Paint the outsides of the two paper bowls gray. Let the paint dry. The bowls will be the monster truck's big wheels.

window

hubcap

truck body

22

This picture of the monster truck shows you how to put all the pieces together. Your truck will make you king of the road!

5 Paste the black hubcaps onto the gray wheels.

6 Paste the black window onto the body of the truck.

7 Paste the wheels and the truck body onto the background cardboard.

8 Stick half of a yellow sticker to the front of the truck for a headlight.

9 Decorate the truck with star stickers.

Bright Ideas!
- Use aluminum foil or silver cardboard to make the hubcaps and the window.
- Decorate your truck by pasting on your own designs or shapes cut out of colored paper.

Hot–Air Balloon

You will need:

- yellow, red, and orange paper or cardboard
- corrugated paper
- brown paint
- paintbrush
- blue background cardboard
- thick, black felt-tip marker

1 Cut a semicircle out of yellow paper or cardboard.

2 Cut another semicircle, the same size, out of red paper or cardboard.

3 Cut a strip of orange paper or cardboard as long as the width of the semicircles.

4 Cut a simple basket shape out of corrugated paper.

5 Paint the corrugated basket brown. Let the paint dry.

top of balloon

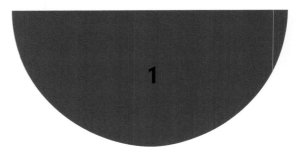

bottom of balloon

middle of balloon

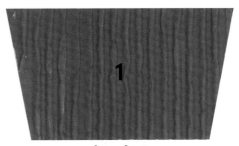

basket

This picture of the balloon shows how the pieces fit together. Your balloon is ready to fly up, up, and away in the bright blue sky!

Bright Ideas!
- Decorate the balloon with stickers or paste on pieces of colored cardboard or tissue paper.
- Use colored yarn for the ropes.

6 Paste the yellow semicircle at the top of the blue background cardboard. Paste the red semicircle directly below it. Paste the orange strip over the line where the semicircles come together.

7 Paste the corrugated paper basket near the bottom of the background cardboard.

8 Use a felt-tip pen to draw in the ropes. Use a ruler to help you make the lines straight.

Delivery Truck

- light blue, dark blue, white, and black paper or cardboard
- background cardboard (any color)
- scraps of paper, tissue paper, or crepe paper in many different colors
- 3 large, round white stickers

cab

window

wheel

1 Cut a large rectangle out of light blue paper or cardboard for the body of the truck.

2 Cut a small rectangle with one sloping side out of dark blue paper or cardboard for the truck's cab.

3 Cut a square window out of white paper or cardboard.

4 Cut three circles out of black paper or cardboard for wheels.

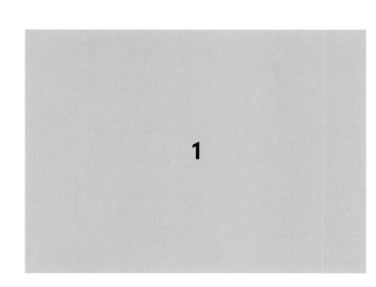

body of truck

26

This picture of the truck shows you how to put the pieces together. Now you can deliver a truck full of treats to all your friends!

5 Paste the body of the truck and the cab onto the background cardboard. Paste the window onto the cab.

6 Decorate the truck by tearing scraps of colored paper, tissue paper, or crepe paper, and then pasting the torn pieces onto the body of the truck.

7 Paste the black wheels onto the truck. Stick a white sticker in the middle of each wheel for hubcaps.

Bright Ideas!
- Make a long truck with an extra trailer and more wheels.
- Decorate your truck with pictures cut out of magazines. This truck is carrying fruits and vegetables.

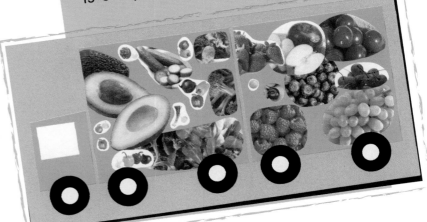

City Bus

- red, black, and white paper or cardboard
- black felt-tip pen
- background cardboard (any color)
- 2 large, round white stickers

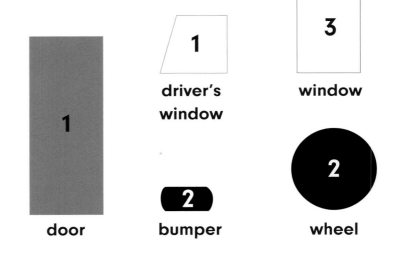

door

driver's window

window

bumper

wheel

1 Draw the bus shape and a long rectangle for a door on red paper or cardboard. Cut out both pieces.

2 Cut two wheels and two bumpers out of black paper or cardboard.

3 Cut three rectangles for windows and one driver's window out of white paper or cardboard.

bus shape

28

This picture of the bus shows how all its pieces should be put together. Is your bus going to school — or to the zoo?

4 Draw a thick black line down the center of the door with a felt-tip pen. Use a ruler to help you make the line straight.

5 Paste the red bus shape onto the background cardboard. Paste the white windows and the red door onto the bus shape. Draw lines around the door with a black felt-tip pen.

6 Paste the black bumpers onto the front and back of the bus.

7 Paste on the black wheels. Stick a white sticker in the center of each wheel to make hubcaps.

Bright Ideas!
- Make a traffic light out of black paper and colored stickers.
- Use aluminum foil or silver cardboard for the bus windows.
- Use colored stickers to add a bus number and a headlight.

Tower Crane

You will need:

- blue and gray paper or cardboard
- background cardboard (any color)
- black felt-tip pen

1 Draw a tower shape, a main arm, and a small arm on blue paper or cardboard. Cut out all three pieces.

2 Draw a small square and a long rectangle on gray paper or cardboard. The rectangle should be wider at one end than the other. Cut out both pieces. The square piece is the crane's weight. The long rectangle is the crane's steel wires.

30

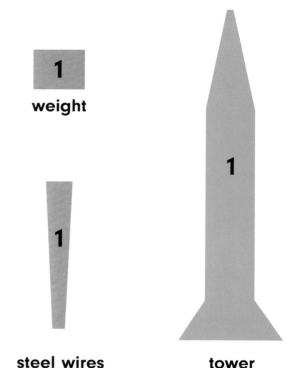

main arm

small arm (1)

weight

steel wires

tower

This picture of the crane shows how to put all the pieces together. What is the heaviest object your crane can lift — a house, an elephant, or something even bigger?

Bright Ideas!
- Make the crane out of silver cardboard or aluminum foil. Use a pencil to draw lines for the steel beams on the tower and the main arm.
- Cut and paint squares of corrugated paper to make crates for the crane to lift.

3 Paste the tower shape and the two arms onto the background cardboard.

4 Paste the square weight under the small arm.

5 Paste the long, gray steel wires under the main arm.

6 Use a black felt-tip pen to draw a big hook at the end of the wires.

 More Craft Books

Cardboard Tube Mania. Craft Mania (series). Christine M. Irvin (Children's Press)

Cut-Paper Play! Dazzling Creations from Construction Paper. Williamson Kids Can! (series). Sandi Henry (Sagebrush)

Paper. Let's Create (series). (Gareth Stevens)

The Super Scissors Book. (Klutz/Chicken Socks)

 Craft Web Sites

Kaboose Crafts
www.kidsdomain.com/craft

Crafts for Kids
www.enchantedlearning.com/crafts

Publisher's note to educators and parents: Our editors have carefully reviewed these Web sites to ensure that they are suitable for children. Many Web sites change frequently, however, and we cannot guarantee that a site's future contents will continue to meet our high standards of quality and educational value. Be advised that children should be closely supervised whenever they access the Internet.